The

LITTLE BOOK OF

FEMINISM

THE LITTLE BOOK OF FEMINISM

Copyright © Summersdale Publishers Ltd, 2016

Research by Abigail McMahon

Illustrations © Shutterstock

Summersdale Publishers Ltd
46 West Street
Chichester
West Sussex
PO19 1RP
UK

www.summersdale.com

Printed and bound in Malta

ISBN: 978-1-84953-844-2

Substantial discounts on bulk quantities of Summersdale books are available to corporations, professional associations and other organisations. For details contact Nicky Douglas by telephone: +44 (0) 1243 756902, fax: +44 (0) 1243 786300 or email: nicky@summersdale.com.

The
LITTLE BOOK OF
FEMINISM

Harriet Dyer

summersdale

CONTENTS

FEMINISM IS DEFINED AS THE 'ADVOCACY OF WOMEN'S RIGHTS ON THE GROUND OF EQUALITY FOR THE SEXES.'

Introduction

Feminism doesn't always mean the same thing to everyone, and that's not surprising; what is a feminist issue for one culture might not apply to another. Given the vast scope of all of human history, it would be impossible to try and fit everything into one 96-page book, even if the writing was very small. Instead, I have chosen to give a brief outline of the history and goals of Western feminism, mainly in the UK, mainland Europe and the US, concentrating specifically on the laws of the UK. Consider this a brief portrait of what feminism has looked like throughout the years, the issues that feminists have focused on and what they have achieved. I hope to demonstrate not only how far we've come but also how far we still have to go in order to achieve true equality. I also hope to point out the issues – subtle and not-so-subtle – still faced by women today.

Statistics

The gender pay gap for people in full-time work in the UK is 10 per cent and in the US it is 21 per cent.

Around 70 per cent of people working minimum-wage jobs are women.

Only 17 per cent of board directors of FTSE 100 companies and 4.6 per cent of Fortune 500 companies are women.

Only one in four MPs is a woman, and women from minority ethnic groups make up only 1.2 per cent of MPs, yet comprise 4 per cent of the UK population.

Just 23 per cent of reporters on national daily newspapers in the UK and 37 per cent in the US are women.

In the US 85 per cent of domestic abuse victims are women and one third of female homicide victims are killed by intimate partners.

Around 85,000 women in the UK and 293,000 women in the US are sexually assaulted each year.

At least 75 per cent of mothers have primary responsibility for childcare in the home.

Almost one in three girls has experienced unwanted sexual touching at school.

One in four women in Britain will experience domestic violence in her lifetime.

Sources: Violence Policy Center, Bureau of Justice Statistics, National Institute of Justice, Center for American Progress, UK Feminista and Refuge UK.

First-Wave

FEMINISM

Introduction

Question: When is a feminist not a feminist? Answer: When she is a first-wave feminist. First-wave feminism is the umbrella term retrospectively applied to the women's rights movement originating in the West in the mid-nineteenth century. However, if you found yourself in the middle of a Langham Place Circle meeting in the 1850s and talked about the feminist cause, you'd get some pretty blank looks, not least for your extraordinary behaviour. The word 'feminist' wasn't in use in Britain until the 1890s. You might get a similar reaction for bandying around the word 'suffragette'. Although almost interchangeable with the term 'first-wave feminist' now, the term suffragette was first used as an insult in 1906 in the *Daily Mail*, a patronisingly feminine twist on the word suffragist, at the time a campaigner for the right to vote. So if first-wave feminists didn't know they were feminists and weren't all suffragists or suffragettes, what were they? What did they want, and what were they for?

The women's rights movement largely consisted of separate groups and independent campaigners working toward improving the rights of women. Although different groups were campaigning for different causes, the main focus was on improving laws and legislation to give women a more equal footing with men. This included better education opportunities, access to certain professions, equal rights in employment, the right to control their own money and property and, of course, the right to vote. For example, the Langham Place Circle campaigned to help women enter the workplace, funding their training (through the unfortunately-named SPEW: The Society for Promoting the Employment of Women) and endeavouring to reduce the social stigma about middle-class women working instead of relying on fathers, brothers and husbands for money. The mid-1800s to the early 1900s saw much change in legislation and women's circumstances.

Boiling Point

In Great Britain in the mid-nineteenth century, women did not have the right to vote, could not as easily divorce their spouses as men could, did not have the right of custody of their children over seven years old, did not have the right to own property if married, could not attend university, could only enter certain professions and – when they were employed – were not afforded equal pay or rights. The law worked in many ways to ensure women's dependence on men.

Such inequality was hardly new for the female population, but by the 1860s conditions were ripe for women to start calling for a better life. A lot of things were changing in British society: by the mid-nineteenth century, the great wave of fresh philosophical thought of the eighteenth-century Enlightenment had provided fertile ground for a drive towards social change throughout society and in 1792, Mary Wollstonecraft published *A Vindication of the Rights of Women*. Men were calling for universal suffrage – the right for all people (or in this case, men) to vote, regardless of personal wealth or status. By the 1830s, slavery had been abolished in Britain and the Chartist movement was fighting for the improvement of working-class political rights. Slowly but surely society's opinions were changing.

There wasn't just philosophical change in the air. In the mid-1800s, the Industrial Revolution was well under way. A leap forward in technology meant a significant change in the lives of working people. Families moved away from the countryside and into the cities for work, changing the typical household set-up known until then. New technology meant that work that used to be performed by skilled workers could now be completed by machines, with factories springing up around the country. Skilled male workers wanted to hold on to their ways of working, fearing they'd be pushed out of the market by automated processes and machines, so withheld their skilled labour from factory owners. These owners, wanting to utilise new machines to maximise profit, consequently hired unskilled women and children to feed the demand for labour. Working-class women found that they worked in similar jobs to men, providing for their families as men did, and yet were not granted the same rights or wages. Women's lives were changing and it was time for Britain's laws to catch up.

VOTES FOR WOMEN

The most famous campaign of first-wave feminism is no doubt the call for votes for women. Even those who aren't experts in the history of feminism (let's be honest, that's most of us) know that in the early 1900s, suffragettes fought for, and eventually obtained, the vote for women in Britain. In fact, history is a little more complicated than that. Suffragettes were the militant branch of the activists campaigning for votes for women, known for disorderly acts of protest, including exploding letterboxes, smashing windows, protesting and, in one incident that exceeds the definition of 'disorderly', blowing up the Chancellor of the Exchequer's house. The suffragettes grew out of the suffragist movement, which campaigned for voting reforms by forming lobbying groups, writing letters and publishing articles, and through bills presented in parliament by male supporters, such as John Stuart Mill. Scornfully referred to as suffragettes in the *Daily Mail*, some female suffragists gleefully took on the name, saying they agreed with the title as they were going to suffra-GET-te the vote. This goes to show that people can be very intelligent and well-meaning and still love bad puns.

Perhaps the most famous suffragette is Emmeline Pankhurst, a figurehead for the movement and founder of the Women's Social and Political Union (WSPU), a powerful force in the campaign for votes for women. She recognised that the suffragist movement's 'quiet' protests hadn't brought women closer to the vote and, in 1903, formed the WSPU, whose approach was 'deeds not words'. It's easy to see how members of the movement were frustrated by their situation: over fifty years of campaigning had not brought about the vote. In 1908, over half a million activists gathered in Hyde Park to call for votes for women; the government took little notice. From 1909, British protest groups intensified their tactics. Women were being taken to prison for their actions and Pankhurst called for hunger strikes in prison to further their protest, taking part in them herself. Suffragette tactics also included property damage, vandalism and attacks on those MPs they saw as obstructing their path to the vote. These extreme tactics certainly brought public attention to the campaign for votes for women, although they caused divided feelings amongst members of the public and the suffragist and suffragette movements alike. Some saw the damage and violence as proof that women were too irrational to be responsible for the vote, while others felt that violence and vandalism were unacceptable in any circumstance. However, in 1914 World War One broke out and, in the face of this national danger, activists suspended their campaign for women's suffrage. After the war ended in 1918, the Representation of the People Act finally gave the vote to all men over 21 and all women over 30.

Landmark Acts

→ **The Married Women's Property Act 1882:** Before this act, a woman's property was transferred to her husband upon marriage and her legal identity ceased to exist. This was because men and women became one when they were married, with the woman subjugated to the man. The act forced the law to recognise a husband and wife as two legal identities, meaning the wife had the right to buy, own and sell her own property. Women also gained the right to sue and be sued, a more thrilling prospect than it might sound.

→ **1913 Cat and Mouse Act:** Seeking to thwart the impact of hunger-striking suffragettes, the act allowed temporary release of weakened and ill prisoners, only for them to be returned to prison once they had regained their strength.

→ **Representation of the People Act 1918:** A landmark development for the voting rights of men and a solid first step for the rights of women, this act abolished all property conditions for men over the age of 21 and awarded women over the age of 30 the right to vote.

The requirement that the voter had to own property still applied to women.

→ **Parliamentary (Qualification of Women) Act 1918:** At 27 words, the UK's shortest statute allowed women over the age of 21 to stand for parliament. To quote it in its entirety, 'A woman shall not be disqualified by sex or marriage for being elected to or sitting or voting as a Member of the Commons House of Parliament.'

→ **Sex Disqualification (Removal) Act 1919:** Following the introduction of votes for women, this act targeted both broad sex discrimination and opened up specific professions and responsibilities. It allowed women onto juries, into the civil service, to work as solicitors and to be admitted to any university, regardless of their marital status.

→ **Representation of the People (Equal Franchise) Act 1928:** Women's voting rights were brought in line with men's with this act – the voting age was lowered to 21 and minimum property requirements were abolished, just as they had been for men.

With their focus on higher education, access to the professions and civil service, and social acceptance of middle-class women entering the workforce, first-wave feminists are now often criticised for having mainly acted in the interests of the middle classes. The campaign for votes for women was more inclusive as it had roots in socialist theory and working-class women's groups strongly contributed to the cause. However, it seems that although working-class women worked with middle-class women at this time, they were ultimately shut out from the upper echelons and leadership positions of the bigger campaigning groups. For example, only one working-class woman, Annie Kenney, ever entered the senior ranks of the WSPU.

History, too, has not been kind to the women of colour and working-class women of first-wave feminism, often removing them from the story altogether. While it is true that the non-white proportion of the British population was smaller in Britain during the mid-nineteenth to early twentieth century than it is today, this doesn't mean there weren't any suffragettes of colour. For example, the Women's Coronation Procession in 1911 featured suffragettes from India, South Africa and the West Indies. The near-non-existence of Sophia Duleep Singh in the history books is a real shame and oversight – princess, activist and goddaughter of Queen Victoria, she sold suffragette newspapers outside Hampton Court Palace and was branded a 'harridan law breaker'.

Probably the biggest criticism of first-wave feminism is that it never actually succeeded in securing women the vote. Suffragette activities were suspended at the outbreak of World War One, with Emmeline Pankhurst calling for all militant activities to stop and for energies to be redirected towards fighting the enemy. Some historians say that it was the work that women did in the war that led to the vote, rather than the previous campaigns by activists and suffragettes. Others claim that the suffragettes' militant activities harmed, rather than helped, their cause, alienating people who were sympathetic and leading politicians to proclaim distrust in women with the vote because of their violent actions (rather conveniently forgetting men's history of violence and war).

BESSIE RAYNER PARKES

Bessie Rayner Parkes was a front-runner of feminist activism in the nineteenth century. Born into a house of liberal values and ideas, she enjoyed a fairly comprehensive education at a Unitarian boarding school. Active from a young age, she published *Remarks on the Instruction of Girls* when she was 25, finding the standard of girls' education, unsurprisingly wanting. Her good friend Barbara Leigh Smith published *A Brief Summary of the Laws in England Concerning Women* at the same time, and this prompted an attempt in 1857 to introduce an act to ensure that women kept control of their property. Parkes and Smith had formed a committee dedicated to lobbying for the act; although unsuccessful, it led to their developing the feminist publication, *The English Woman's Journal*.

As well as contributing many articles on topical political and social issues to the journal, Parkes was also one of its editors and shareholders. The journal engaged with many feminist activities, including highlighting the stigma faced by single women who, although considered middle-class, had to work to support themselves or else face dire financial circumstances. It argued that the veneer of gentility was not worth a life of poverty and urged other women who did not have to face that predicament to support their sisters.

Working on the journal gave Parkes, Smith and other activists a safe space to discuss their political ideas at its offices, 19 Langham Place. They became known as The Langham Place Group, the first organisation to campaign for a woman's right to vote alongside its crusades for adequate education, employment opportunities and property rights. It is considered by some to be the first organised women's movement in Britain.

Parkes was active all her life, and was also known as a poet and author, counting John Ruskin among her admirers.

'IF IT IS RIGHT FOR MEN TO FIGHT FOR THEIR FREEDOM, AND GOD KNOWS WHAT THE HUMAN RACE WOULD BE LIKE TODAY IF MEN HAD NOT, SINCE TIME BEGAN, FOUGHT FOR THEIR FREEDOM, THEN IT IS RIGHT FOR WOMEN TO FIGHT FOR THEIR FREEDOM AND THE FREEDOM OF THE CHILDREN THEY BEAR.'

EMMELINE PANKHURST

'IF WOMEN BE EDUCATED FOR DEPENDENCE; THAT IS, TO ACT ACCORDING TO THE WILL OF ANOTHER FALLIBLE BEING, AND SUBMIT, RIGHT OR WRONG, TO POWER, WHERE ARE WE TO STOP?'

MARY WOLLSTONECRAFT

In a Nutshell

WE WANT!

Improved property rights for women

Social acceptance of middle-class women
supporting themselves in work

Equal pay for working-class women
already in work

Votes for women

Better education for girls of all classes

Acceptance into all universities for all degrees

The legal ability to work in all professions, including law and politics

Female members of parliament

Associated movements: anti-slavery, socialism, suffragist

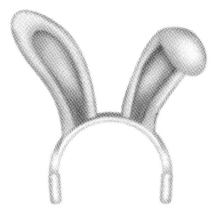

Second-Wave

FEMINISM

Introduction

By the end of the 1920s, women were enjoying many of the rights they had long campaigned for, and it's probably reasonable to guess that they thought things would just keep getting better. However, within a short decade, the world had become involved in World War Two. Afterwards, with everyone desperate to return to a normal society that they could never regain and that perhaps hadn't existed in the first place, more conservative values crept into society and the media. Femininity was again paramount and women's places were once more in the home.

Then the sixties swept in and with it the sexual revolution and the start of second-wave feminism in America, known as the women's liberation movement. A wave of increasingly liberal attitudes swept society; drug-taking, long hair, rock music, increasingly rebellious teenagers breaking away from the drab conformism they identified with their parents' generation and... sex. People were not only having sex but *talking* about it, and women were coming up with some pointers for improvement. Traditionally, a woman's sexuality was tangled up with societal pressure not to have sex and a lack of available contraception, leading to a raft of problems including social judgement if she did have sex. If a woman got past these obstacles, she often found that her own sexual pleasure was sidelined in favour of her male partner's.

It wasn't just in the bedroom that women were dissatisfied. By the 1970s, despite considerable social advancement, women could still be (and were) paid less than a man while in the same job, sexual harassment was known only as a 'bit of harmless fun' and posts were advertised by gender.

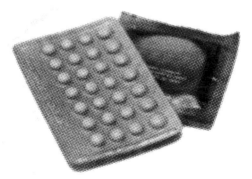

In the years following World War Two, America struggled to re-establish 'normality' in the wake of the turmoil and tragedy it had suffered. Although understandable, this led to a kind of societal over-correction, with gender roles being more firmly entrenched than ever before and domesticity returning to the centre of many women's lives. Meanwhile, in France, Simone de Beauvoir published her philosophical text *The Second Sex*, which discussed the fallacy of women's inferiority to men and which had previously been justified by their biological differences. (Women have been battling myths about the inferiority of their bodies for thousands of years, from the idea that crops would die in the presence of a menstruating woman to the fear that their wombs would fly out if they travelled on a train). De Beauvoir also explored the historical and social factors involved in women's positions, moving on from the legislative concerns of first-wave feminism and setting the tone for second-wave feminism.

In 1961 the contraceptive pill was introduced to the US and Britain. This gave women more control over whether they had children, which meant they had more control over their bodies as well as their careers. Then 1963 arrived, thought to be the tipping point in generating the second wave of feminist activism. Betty Friedan wrote *The Feminine Mystique*, criticising how women were depicted in the media and the waste of women's potential by limiting their sphere to the home. Also in this year, John F. Kennedy's administration commissioned and published 'The Presidential Commission on the Status of Women', which highlighted that legislation that had meant to 'protect' women due to 'biological' differences had actually led to employers avoiding hiring women in the first place or paying them equal wages.

Towards the end of the sixties and the start of the seventies, the feminist thinking of the US was spilling out into the rest of the world, particularly into the UK. In 1967, British women gained further control over their bodies with the Abortion Act being passed, and, in 1968, women at the Ford automobile plant in Dagenham went on strike for equal pay. For the next decade, feminist activists and thinkers raised awareness and campaigned for not only equal rights in the workplace but also a change in perspective of women's bodies and sexuality.

THE PERSONAL IS POLITICAL

The phrase 'The personal is political' was popularised by a 1969 essay by Carol Hanisch, although she denies originating the phrase herself. It is a handy summing up of the arguments of second-wave feminists: personal experience and problems have political origins and solutions. Issues that women faced concerning sex, contraception, abortion, appearance, childcare and division of labour in the home were not just each woman's personal problem but something that stemmed from historical and social issues and could be solved with increased awareness and changes in legislation and policy.

One example of this is Germaine Greer's 1970 book *The Female Eunuch*. She argued that there was no difference between the brain of a man and that of a woman and that it was the traditional nuclear family that oppressed women. She said that society taught women self-imposed limitations (e.g. through emphasis on motherhood and 'ladylike' behaviour) and that by limiting their place in society, both men and women were taught subconsciously to hate women. She said the freedom she was looking for was 'Freedom to run, shout, talk loudly and sit with your knees apart.'

By adopting 'the personal is political' as their mantra, second-wave feminists made it acceptable to talk about these issues. It meant they weren't dismissed as private problems but could be used to analyse why we think certain things about how a woman should behave and whether those things are actually true, or whether they come from long-held assumptions. It also meant problems based in the home could be combatted by the law: in 1976, the Domestic Violence and Matrimonial Proceedings Act meant people could seek legal protection against a violent spouse or partner, criminalising domestic abuse.

→ **Abortion Act 1967:** Abortion became legal for women in the UK (excluding Northern Ireland) on the condition that it took place at under 24 weeks, two doctors had advised the woman and that continuing the pregnancy would be harmful to either the woman or child's physical health or the woman's mental health. This law is still active today.

→ **Equal Pay Act 1970:** Although passed in 1970, women had to wait another five years for this act to come into force. It worked to ensure there was no difference between a man and woman's pay or conditions of employment as long as the work they did was the same or is of equal value.

→ **Employment Protection Act 1975:** Reviewing workers rights, this act made it illegal to fire a woman because she is pregnant and introduced 'statutory maternity provision' (companies must provide maternity leave).

→ **Sexual Offences (Amendment) Act 1976:** This act 'upgraded' rape from a common law offence to give it a statutory – i.e. legal – definition, essentially criminalising it. Sadly, non-consensual sex within a marriage wasn't included in the definition, being regarded as more of a 'failure of marriage' than a crime.

→ **Domestic Violence and Matrimonial Proceedings Act 1976**: Criminalising domestic abuse, this enabled victims to take out restraining orders against their attacker even if they were married to them. It also criminalised sexual abuse in a marriage and meant the attacker could be removed from a home if they shared it with their victim.

Criticism

Second-wave feminism wasn't the only feminist movement growing out of the sixties. The decade also saw the rise of radical feminism, sharing many of the same concerns about a woman's place in the home, at work, sexual objectification and amount of reproductive control. However, some of these views are taken to a more extreme and, some would say, black-and-white view. For example, a famous radical feminist perspective is that pornography is the eroticisation of women's humiliation and coercion, and so pornography is tantamount to rape. They would argue that even if a female porn artist thought that she chose the profession, or a woman thought she enjoyed watching porn, this was a result of society's brainwashing rather than 'truth'. As with many criticisms of radical feminist theories, modern critics say this is patronising and sex-shaming; it dismisses the idea that women can refuse to be objectified but still enjoy sex and watching porn.

Radical feminists' theories on transgender women have long been controversial, too. While second-wave and radical feminists created strong alliances with lesbian and gay causes, their relationship with transgender people has tended to be less welcoming. Some feminists saw men transitioning to women not as a personal expression of 'true self' but as a way for men to step on a space meant for women. The debate is complex, ongoing and has involved less than dignified comments that only serve to muddy the dialogue.

Second-wave feminists' emphasis on the personal being political has also lead to the exclusion of other minorities. Many of the important texts of the movement were written by white, middle-class women – *The Second Sex*, *The Feminine Mystique*, *The Female Eunuch* – and this meant the experiences portrayed were specific to their race and class. Black feminists argue that these experiences are not always the same as their own, as they also have issues of racism to contend with on top of sexism. bell hooks' *Ain't I a Woman*, published in 1981, asserted that the feminist movement had ignored the non-white, non-middle-class experience, reinforcing sexism, racism and classism.

GLORIA STEINEM

Active in the civil rights movement and a staunch anti-Vietnam-war campaigner, American activist Gloria Steinem first came to national attention with her article on life as a Playboy bunny, 'A Bunny's Tale'. She was hired as a bunny and wrote a piece exposing the exploitative working conditions. She undermined the idea that the sexual revolution was benefitting men and women alike, highlighting the disrespect and financial cheating the bunnies received by both colleagues and clients.

Steinem wrote other pieces that were on the hot button of second-wave feminist interests, such as when she covered an abortion 'speak out' in 1969 or wrote the satirical essay 'If Men Could Menstruate' for *Cosmopolitan*. She founded *Ms* magazine in 1972 upon realising that there 'really was nothing for women to read that was controlled by women'. Over the years, the magazine has covered diverse topics such as sweatshops, sex trafficking and date rape, and it was the first national magazine in the US to discuss domestic violence. She was also highly involved in politics, supporting several politicians over the years (including both Hillary Clinton and Barack Obama) and founded the National Woman's Political Caucus in the seventies, dedicated to supporting and training women who wish to seek elected and appointed offices. Steinem is still politically active today, joining Women's Walk for Peace, an international group seeking the reunification of Korea.

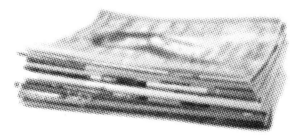

BETTY FRIEDAN

Friedan's *The Feminine Mystique* is one of the texts said to have sparked the second-wave feminist movement. She had both worked as a journalist, being fired upon falling pregnant with her second child, and had lived as a homemaker. The book reflected her own experiences and pointed out the sacrifices women made in order to fulfil gender expectations and become a homemaker to a husband's breadwinner. Often sacrificing their own education and trapped in repetitive daily routines, Friedan argued that women were left dissatisfied in the life of a suburban homemaker.

She co-founded the National Organisation for Women, which fought for women's rights in the workplace and is still active to this day. She accused the media of attempting to ridicule the women's rights movement by focussing on issues such as whether or not to wear bras (even today a woman daring to point out something is sexist often has to suffer through a groan-worthy 'burn your bras' joke).

'I THINK THE PERSON WHO SAID: "HONEY, IF MEN COULD GET PREGNANT, ABORTION WOULD BE A SACRAMENT" WAS RIGHT.'

GLORIA STEINEM

'AS [THE HOUSEWIFE] MADE THE BEDS, SHOPPED FOR GROCERIES ... SHE WAS AFRAID TO ASK EVEN OF HERSELF THE SILENT QUESTION – "IS THIS ALL?"'

BETTY FRIEDAN

WE WANT!

Girls to be supported in having a dream
other than 'being a housewife'

Not to be discriminated against in the workplace,
to be treated as peers by male colleagues

Equal pay

Maternity rights, including not being
fired for being pregnant

Body autonomy, including access to contraception
and decreased stigma surrounding abortion

To stop the sexual objectification of women,
including banning pornography

Better services and protection for
domestic abuse and rape victims

**Associated movements: civil rights,
gay rights, the sexual revolution**

Third-Wave

FEMINISM

Introduction

By the 1990s, some of the views and positions of second-wave feminism were facing a backlash, which eventually developed into the movement known as third-wave feminism. Highly critical of the way the feminist movement had mainly seemed to serve white, middle-class women, third-wave feminists were keen to let diverse women tell their own unique stories. Their thinking was that feminism had to represent *all* types of women, actively including those of all colours, ethnicities, religions, occupations and sexualities.

Feminism has always enjoyed strong links with socialism and anti-capitalist movements. With third-wave feminism this connection took shape through association with the riot grrrl subculture, a movement with anti-corporate and punk values. Placing importance on the adolescent girl's standpoint, the riot grrrl movement included home-made 'zines, political action, bands and activism.

Third-wave feminists continued their predecessors' work on raising awareness about the issues of rape and domestic violence and how the political system could work harder to protect victims of both those issues.

They were also interested in reversing some of the strict black and white regulations of second-wave feminists, preferring to reclaim issues that had previously been seen as problematic rather than brand them 'antifeminist'. For example, they attempted to give words like 'bitch' a positive, powerful connotation, preferring to subvert the meaning in an empowering way rather than to censor the word itself.

Boiling Point

Second-wave feminists had seen many political victories, and by the nineties many people thought that the legal system was now largely fair to both genders. While there were still battles to be won in that arena, more and more feminists were turning their attention to social change on a smaller scale, such as reclaiming language, defeating stereotypes and changing media depiction of women.

Although clearly influenced by second-wave feminism's mantra that 'the personal is political', third-wave feminism wanted to move away from the prescriptive attitudes of its predecessors and towards the idea of freedom to choose. Previously topics such as porn or gender had strict dos and don'ts for what was good for women. For example, pornography was always seen to be oppressing the woman, even if the woman thought she wanted to partake in or watch it. This particular debate was fought in the rather gloriously named 'feminist sex wars' (also known by the similarly flamboyant title of 'porn wars'). The boiled-down argument focussed on whether a woman, living in a patriarchal society where she is nurtured to think a certain way about how women should behave and please men, could ever be able truly to make an independent decision to participate in porn. Some also felt that second-wave feminists' criticisms about sexual oppression actually themselves oppressed women. For example, second-wave feminists discredited the idea that a woman could genuinely enjoy sadomasochism, refuting the idea that it could be participated in healthily and be a natural, personal kink.

Works such as bell hooks' *Ain't I a Woman* and Maxine Hong Kingston's *The Woman Warrior* had explored the possibilities for the discussion of race in combination with gender. Queer theory was rising to prominence and its rejection of simply two genders – man and woman – and two sexualities – gay and straight – meant that the more binary views of sexuality in second-wave feminism were now also in need of updating.

QUEER THEORY

Coined as a term in 1990 by feminist academic Teresa de Lauretis, queer theory placed assumptions about sexuality and gender under the microscope. Feminism had already cast a light on the idea of 'natural' gender behaviour, with many key arguments hinging on the idea that women aren't in the oppressed position they're in because of natural weakness or inferiority. Instead, research has shown that women have the biological potential to be equal to men in many ways, but social norms, laws and lack of opportunity have stood in their way. Studies introduced ideas such as the theory that parents pushing their children to play with gendered toys meant children learned to act a certain way according to whether they were a boy or a girl, which was then taken to mean they were 'naturally' feminine/masculine.

Queer theory took that idea to the next level. The name itself is typical of third-wave feminism. Traditionally used as a slur, queer theorists repurposed the word 'queer' as an umbrella term to mean 'different to the sex and gender norm'. Queer theory meant that if gender and sexuality weren't predetermined, then people of any gender didn't *have* to act in a certain way, according to whether they were a man or woman. This meant there could be space between who someone is and what they do/how they behave.

As well as adding to the developing idea that a person could be feminist and still partake in activities that had previously been thought to objectify women, as long as they did it with full awareness of context and free will, queer theory also opened the way for transwomen to be accepted in the feminist movement. If gender was no longer simply defined as a biological trait, then it became easier to accept that a person could identify as female even if she was born biologically male.

Landmark Acts

→ **Finance Act 1998:** This act introduced a new means of taxation known as Independent Taxation and was applicable from 1990 onwards. Previously, a married couple had been aggregated and then taxed based on the husband's income, with responsibility for taxes also falling on the husband. The change in law meant that, although married, the husband and wife were now treated as two separate entities.

→ **Ending the marital law rape exemption, 1991:** It is shocking to think it was as recently as 1991 in England and Wales (1989 in Scotland) that by definition rape couldn't take place within a marriage, even if the couple were separated and one member had a Family Protection Order against their spouse. Thankfully, a case of this nature was instrumental in leading to the exemption being repealed and rape within a marriage being made illegal.

→ ***The Vagina Monologues*, 1996**: A play by Eve Ensler, consisting of several monologues written about the female experience and read out by different female actors. Christopher Isherwood called it the 'most important piece of political theatre of the last decade.' It raised awareness for topics such as rape camps, menstruation and childbirth. However, the play has also been the subject of criticism, with an act that portrays the statutory rape of a thirteen-year-old girl by an older woman in a positive light.

→ **General Election, 1997**: The number of female MPs doubled from 60 to 120. Earlier in 1992, Betty Boothroyd had taken the role as first female speaker of the House of Commons. Labour engineered this sudden jump in female MPs with an all-women shortlist – a hot issue in modern gender politics.

While third-wave feminism opened up the movement to welcome everyone, some felt that this left feminism without a clear aim. While it was easy to associate first- and second-wave feminism with a number of clearly defined issues, for some third-wave feminism was seen by some as more nebulous and less driven. Where it did have clear aims, such as improving media representation or an increasing in women's shelters, some critics argued that these were simply extensions of second-wave feminism and that the third wave couldn't be clearly defined as its own movement.

As with any movement that encompasses many different people from many different walks of life, feminism became many different things with different aims. This could also give the impression of a movement that didn't know what it wanted: if one group of feminists was arguing for one solution, another could be found that was firmly against it. However, feminism has always had its internal divisions, from the days of the Pankhurst family to the present, and many see it as a welcome cost of inclusivity.

Third wave's accepting 'if you choose to do it, it's empowering' attitude led some to feel it was actually contributing to the harmful sexualisation and objectification of women. The flip side of accepting any free-will action as feminist meant the context in which the action occurred wasn't criticised – if feminists acted exactly the way society had been nurturing women to act, could they truly be feminist? Even small actions such as wearing make up or heels came up for fierce debate. Media and society pressure women to look a certain way; when feminists conform to this but say they're doing it for themselves rather than others, are they really making their own choices or acting according to their conditioning?

Feminist Heroine

NAOMI WOLF

Naomi Wolf is an American journalist and author considered to be a spokesperson for third-wave feminism. Her book *The Beauty Myth* was published in 1991 to widespread acclaim. The idea central to the text was that women are held to impossible beauty standards and that even as they gain social and economic power, the pressure to appear a certain way weighs more heavily on them. Wolf highlighted the repercussions incurred by women who didn't conform to imposed standards, citing, for example, the rise in recorded numbers of eating-disorder sufferers over the years. Wolf said that, 'A culture fixated on female thinness is not an obsession about female beauty, but an obsession about female obedience.' Wolf's findings in *The Beauty Myth* didn't go unchallenged, however; Christina Hoff Summers disputed Wolf's claim that 150,000 women were dying yearly from anorexia, and Camille Paglia fiercely criticised Wolf's research and analysis. Paglia, who does not fear confrontation with fellow feminists, and Wolf took their debate to the pages of the *New Republic*, where they continued their heated, and sometimes personal, argument. Wolf has continued in her activism, publishing books and articles and campaigning, including being arrested in 2011 while participating in the Occupy Wall Street movement.

'THE CONNECTIONS BETWEEN AND AMONG WOMEN ARE THE MOST FEARED, THE MOST PROBLEMATIC, AND THE MOST POTENTIALLY TRANSFORMING FORCE ON THE PLANET.'

ADRIENNE RICH

'RIOTS NOT DIETS.'

ANONYMOUS

WE WANT!

Sexual freedom to enjoy and participate
in sex, pornography and BDSM

To reclaim and subvert slurs and insulting
words, such as 'bitch' or 'slut'

Better domestic abuse facilities, such
as more women's shelters

Improved representation in the media

Improved representation in politics, including
higher numbers of female MPs

Associated movements: In place of associating with other movements, third-wave feminism tried to incorporate them, including black feminism and queer theory as well as transgender rights

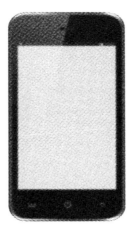

Today's

FEMINISM

Introduction

Feminism today continues the work and builds on the theories of third-wave feminism. There is debate as to whether this is simply a continuation of third-wave feminism or whether, after a relatively quiet period during the 'noughties', growing public participation in the ideals of feminism indicates that this could be considered a fourth wave.

The aims of modern feminism are similar to those of the third wave: sex and body positivity, that old (yet elusive) workhorse of equal pay, a change in gender norms and a greater focus on prevention of domestic abuse and sexual assault. However, today's campaigns reflect the unique problems faced by women in the new technological age, even as the root problems of sexism, misogyny and inequality remain unchanged. Cyber-bullying and underrepresentation of women in video games are just two of these very modern issues.

The media also continues to act as a channel for feminists to campaign for improved rights in addition to being a problem in and of itself. Cartoonist Alison Bechdel's eponymous Bechdel-Wallace Test, created in the mid-eighties, poses a seemingly easy challenge to pass in modern times; the only criteria are that a film has two or more female characters, that they are named, that they talk to each other and that they discuss something other than a man. However, 2014 saw a massive drop in films passing the Bechdel test, from 67 per cent in 2013 down to 55 per cent. If women reach for the loftier heights of films featuring women in the lead role, they find even more meagre offerings; only 29 per cent of films had female protagonists; pretty scanty representation of a group that represents unchangingly 50 per cent of the world's population.

Today's feminism also continues the battle for better protection for victims of rape and sexual assault. Despite an ever-increasing number of studies into the causes of rape, there still appears to be a worrying trend for male politicians to say stupid and frankly untrue things about sexual assault and the female victims of it. In 2011, Kenneth Clarke, worryingly the British Justice Secretary at the time, caused upset when he differentiated between 'date rape' and 'serious rape'. In 2012, in the US,

Republican Senate candidate Todd Aikin asserted that women couldn't get pregnant as a result of rape, claiming that 'the female body has ways to shut that whole thing down'. Also in 2012, in India, after an internationally notorious crime where a young women was gang-raped to death on a bus, spiritual guru Asaram Bapu claimed the victim was in part responsible for her own attack, as she could have prevented it had she 'chanted God's name'. These perspectives are deeply worrying, especially as they were spoken by people in positions of power whose responsibility should be towards victims and the prevention of crimes, and are indicative of a culture that still assumes women provoke their own sexual attacks.

Boiling Point

The accelerated rate of technological development and the internet has led to specific feminist issues arising that hadn't been explored in previous waves. Feminists have highlighted the higher rate of abusive and threatening messages received online by women in comparison to men, bringing attention to the poor infrastructure that internet companies and policing institutions have at their disposal to tackle these problems. Cyber-bullying can take many forms, from insulting comments and 'trolling' in the comments section of a female journalist's online article, to sexually aggressive and offensive messages women receive on online dating sites and apps. While online culture has developed a certain element of unpleasant behaviour, such as 'trolling', succinctly defined by *Urban Dictionary* as 'Being a prick on the internet just because you can', studies have found that men receive internet abuse for a variety of reasons but rarely simply for being men. Women, however, are often targeted by gender-specific and sexually aggressive slurs and threats.

The accelerated nature of technology means that law enforcement has struggled to keep up and fails to react effectively to problems that no one could have predicted, such as revenge porn, a particularly nasty practice of placing photos of women, taken with the understanding that they were private, on the internet to shame and humiliate them, usually by an aggrieved ex-partner. The international nature of the online environment also means that it can be hard to prosecute crimes; in 2014, Apple's iCloud was hacked and hundreds of photos of famous women circulated. The speed at which the photos were disseminated around the world made it difficult for prosecutors to target any one particular criminal. Given the intangible nature of the crime of hacking, combined with the public profile of the women involved, many people viewed the photos with the assumption that it was an acceptable consequence of putting your photos on a cloud drive. The women themselves disputed this mindset, pleading with people not to look at their personal photos, stating it made them feel violated.

SLUT WALK

In 2011, a Toronto police officer addressing college students made the remark that 'women should avoid dressing like sluts' in order to prevent sexual assault. In April of that year, as a response, the first Slutwalk was organised in Toronto and the practice quickly spread around the world, in protest of the idea that a woman's clothes can incite sexual assault.

Feminists and those who work with sexual assault victims and perpetrators reject the idea that a woman's clothes contribute to assaults, pointing to the many attacks that take place when the victim is 'covered up' or in countries where women are veiled. Even defining women as 'covered up' is challenging, as those who claim that revealing clothing incites assault have yet to release the definitive percentage of skin to be covered in order for a woman to be safe from sexual assault (because there isn't one).

Although this theory was already a standard element of training for people in professions that dealt with attacks, such as police officers, lawyers and judges, the Toronto officer's comments highlighted that many professionals thought otherwise, which is dangerous for the victims that rely on them for help. It also reflected society's opinion on sexual assault. Defined by feminists as 'rape culture', this is the societal assumption that a woman presents herself as available and interested in sex merely by being in the presence of a man, regardless of what they say or indicate through body language.

Slutwalks take a similar format to other feminist marches, such as Take Back The Night protests, which raise awareness of the effect of violence in limiting the places a woman can go and the hours during which she should travel. As organised marches, they feature placards, chanted slogans and talks to raise awareness of issues surrounding female sexuality and safety.

→ **Equality Act 2010:** The Equality Act 2010 clarified the procedures and definitions surrounding discrimination in the workplace. For example, pay secrecy was now no longer enforceable, meaning that women could properly assess their pay in relation to their male colleagues.

→ **Shared Parental Leave, 2015:** This amendment to maternity and paternity legislation meant that parents could share an allowance of 50 weeks paid leave as they wished, expanding men's rights to paternity leave past their previous two weeks paid-leave period. This gives them greater opportunity to be involved with childcare at the newborn stage and takes the burden off mothers to be sole caretakers in the first year.

→ **Criminal and Justice Courts Bill amendment 2015:** The relatively sudden rise of technology meant legal loopholes rendered 'revenge porn' almost un-prosecutable, as the photos would often be considered the perpetrator's property, as they were previously given to them, regardless of the wishes of the victim at the present time. The amendment introduced the necessitation of consent – the subject of the photo had to consent to it being shared, whether it was privately or online. Violation of the amendment can result in up to two years in prison.

→ **2015 Saudi Arabian Municipal Elections:** In 2011 King Abdullah announced that women would be able to register to vote and stand as candidates in the next election, due to be held in 2015. This was a landmark announcement, as Saudi Arabia was the last country in the world to have a gender-specific ban on political suffrage. In August of 2015, 131,000 women registered to vote and around 18 women were elected to council positions.

Feminist Heroines

It's tricky to analyse objectively a person's influence without the benefit of hindsight, so here are a few spotlights on women who are generally kicking ass and taking names at the moment.

CAITLIN MORAN

Heralding the renewed interest in feminist issues with her book *How to Be a Woman*, Moran argues for women to be less self-critical and self-limiting and to ignore the pressures to behave in a certain way from the media and society. Her outlook on feminism is potentially more appealing to all genders as she believes that it isn't about being good to women specifically, it's just basic politeness. Essentially, she argues for female happiness!

CHIMAMANDA NGOZI ADICHIE

Critically acclaimed author Ngozi Adichie gave a seminal TED talk, 'We should all be feminists', later published as a book. In it she explored what it meant to be an African feminist and the assumptions she had received not only about her gender but also about her nationality and race. Parts of the talk were sampled in Beyonce's song 'Flawless', bringing her feminist ideals to a wider audience.

LENA DUNHAM

Media personality, author and creator of the American TV series *Girls*, Dunham is a controversial figure, occasionally saying things that not only non-feminists but also feminists find problematic. However, it would be difficult to argue that she shouldn't be credited with the popularisation of feminism and feminist topics, especially in the US.

LAURA BATES

Founder of The Everyday Sexism Project, in which women send in the small, often unnoticed, examples of sexism in their everyday lives. Bates pioneered the use of social media in feminist campaigns, quickly disseminating the examples across the internet, highlighting and placing importance on the smaller struggles women face in their day-to-day lives and allowing women to see that others are struggling with the same problems as them. Her book on the subject, also named *Everyday Sexism*, collates and explores the responses she has received.

EMMA WATSON

Unlike the other women on these pages who rose to fame as feminist activists, Watson is a celebrated actress. A graduate of the prestigious Brown University in the US, Watson has also seen the darker side of fame, after members of the website 4Chan allegedly threatened to release nude photos of her after she spoke out for women's rights. In 2014 she was appointed UN Women Goodwill Ambassador and now campaigns for gender equality around the world. Her starting campaign is HeForShe, an international effort to get men more involved in feminist causes.

'WHAT IS FEMINISM? SIMPLY THE BELIEF THAT WOMEN SHOULD BE AS FREE AS MEN, HOWEVER NUTS, DIM, DELUDED, BADLY DRESSED, FAT, RECEDING, LAZY, AND SMUG THEY MIGHT BE.'

CAITLIN MORAN

'I THINK WOMEN WHO REJECT THE TERM DON'T KNOW WHAT IT MEANS. IT'S NOT A CONCEPT YOU REJECT. IF YOU'RE A FEMINIST, YOU BELIEVE IN EQUAL OPPORTUNITIES.'

LENA DUNHAM

Better protections and resources for domestic
abuse and sexual assault victims

To change society's perceptions on the
causes of rape and 'rape culture'

Better representation for women in the media

Equal pay and working opportunities,
including representation in the top tiers
of business, media and politics

Legislation protecting women against cyber crime

Associated movements: particular campaigns include Tropes vs Women in Video Games, HeforShe, Black Lives Matter and No More Page Three

Feminism

AROUND
THE WORLD

NEW ZEALAND

Maori culture was traditionally matrilineal, although colonial society later dominated the country and established its own cultural norms in place of that of the Maori. However, it may be this factor, in combination with the Kiwis' drive to attract women to move to the country by offering good rates of pay, that led to New Zealand being the first country in the world to award women the vote in 1893. In 2005, New Zealand made history again when it became the first country in the world to have all its highest offices held by women.

INDIA

A perfect example of how Western feminism isn't a copy-and-paste movement that works for all cultures. Western feminism originated from the rise of individualism, while India's culture can value self-denial for the greater good. India is a large country, populated by many religions and different cultures, so a variety of feminist ideologies are needed to accommodate different issues and cultural practices. Early Indian feminism in the nineteenth century saw the Hindu and Sikh practice of 'Sati' (widow immolation) abolished, age of consent regulated and child marriage banned, amongst other progress. Modern Indian feminism addresses issues such as modernisation vs tradition, education opportunities, dress code and autonomy. International attention has been given to cases of sexual assault in India, with some citing it as a particular national issue.

ICELAND

On 24 October 1975, women in Iceland walked out of their homes and jobs to rally in Reykjavik's Down Square. Called the 'Women's Day Off', (or for some of the men left behind 'The Long Friday'), without women working or looking after the children, the country ground to a halt. Credited with changing the way of thinking, five years later Iceland had a female president. Since then, it has introduced paid paternity leave (in 2000) and has topped WEF's Global Gender Gap Index since 2009, with 44 per cent of parliament made up by women.

SAUDI ARABIA

Although there has been a women's rights movement in Saudi Arabia since the sixties, the female population has very few rights compared to Saudi men. The country has received international scrutiny for its illegalisation of female drivers, the fact that all women are required to have a male guardian to make certain legal decisions for them and that women were not able to vote until well into the twenty-first century. After a long battle for suffrage, women were granted the right to vote and run for parliament in 2011. In 2015 that ruling came into effect and women are starting to exercise these rights for the first time.

THE PHILIPPINES

Having granted women the vote in 1937, the Philippines is now ranked as one of the top countries in the world for gender equality. Prior to colonisation, Filipino society gave equal weight to maternal as well as paternal lineage, in addition to giving women the power to divorce their husbands and own their own property. Although women's rights were set back by colonisation and the dissemination of patriarchal Christian values, the Philippines' history of gender parity stood feminist campaigners in good stead to effect social change. The Philippines now ranks fifth among 136 countries on the Gender Gap Index, with Filipino feminists campaigning for, among other causes, greater parity of representation in government.

THE UNITED STATES OF AMERICA

Gender equality in the US is largely comparable to that of the UK. Both countries influenced each other's feminist thinking throughout the years and women gained rights at roughly the same rate. However, there are some areas that are the subject of fierce discussion. The US is the only country considered to be 'developed' that doesn't guarantee paid maternity leave, with women able to exercise the right to 12 weeks' unpaid leave. Surprisingly for the nation that could be described as the birthplace of second-wave feminism, there has also been recent controversy surrounding birth control and abortion, with more than 282 abortion restrictions enacted since 2010, including increases of the required waiting period and the number of times a woman must visit a doctor before an abortion.

Feminist

DICTIONARY

Agency: The ability of people to make their own decisions and control their own actions.

Androcentrism: The placing of men at the centre of a world view, religion or culture.

Axis of Oppression: The four systems by which a person can be oppressed: gender, race, class and sexual orientation.

Bechdel-Wallace Test: A way of testing gender equality in the media. To pass, there need to be two or more female characters in a work of fiction, who are named, who talk to each other and whose subject of conversation is not men. Although this is a good 'spot check' for a film with good gender equality, it by no means guarantees that the movie supports feminist values.

Cisgender: A person whose birth gender matches the gender with which they identify.

Gender: A male or female status or identification.

Heteronormative: The placing of heterosexual orientation at the centre of a world view, religion or culture.

Intersectionality: The interconnected nature of social categorizations such as race, class, and gender as they apply to a given individual or group, regarded as creating overlapping and interdependent systems of discrimination or disadvantage.

Kink-shaming: To devalue a person because of their sexual interests or fetishes, known as 'kinks'.

Male gaze theory: That art, advertising and created objects are created with the assumption that a man is viewing them.

Mansplain: A condescending explanation by a man to a woman, often on a topic about which the woman is knowledgeable.

Misandry: An ingrained distrust or hatred of the male gender.

Misogyny: An ingrained distrust or hatred of the female gender.

MRA: An acronym spelling 'Men's rights activist'.

Not All Men: A phrase sometimes used by men to dismiss gendered discussions such as those surrounding domestic violence or sexual assault. Now also used as a feminist hashtag to mock that dismissal.

Objectification: One person seeing or treating another as less than human or as an object, usually in a sexual manner.

Othering: Treating another person or group as alien to oneself because of difference, for example, gender, class, race or sexual orientation.

Patriarchy: A society, organisation or system in which men have more power, and sometimes rights, than women.

Privilege: An advantage or special right granted to one person or group and denied to others.

Rape culture: A society that places the blame, implicitly or explicitly, of sexual assault on the victims and normalises sexual violence.

Sexism: Prejudice against one gender.

Slut-shaming: To devalue or criticise a person, usually a woman, because of sexual activity.

Suffragette: Originally meant as a slur, a woman seeking equal rights, including the right to vote.

Suffragist: A person seeking equal political rights, including the right to vote.

Terf: Acronym for 'Trans-exclusionary radical feminist'; considered a subgroup of radical feminism and characterised by hostility to the inclusionary views of third-wave feminism. They believe in classic binary gender division, i.e. a woman is someone who is born with a vagina and XX chromosomes.

Victim blaming: Assigning the fault to the victim of a crime rather than to the perpetrator of it.

Womanism: Feminism that allows for the perspective and experience of women of colour.

Womyn: A feminist spelling of 'woman' to avoid the suffix of 'man'.

Reading

LIST

A Vindication of the Rights of Woman, Mary Wollstonecraft (1792)

A Brief Summary of Laws Concerning Women, Barbara Leigh-Smith Bodichon (1854)

Remarks on the Education of Girls, with Reference to the Social, Legal, and Industrial Position of Women in the Present Day, Bessie Rayner Parkes (1856)

The Subjection of Women, John Stuart Mill (1869)

The Origin of the Family, Private Property and the State, Friedrich Engels (1884)

The Awakening, Kate Chopin (1899)

A Room of One's Own, Virginia Woolf (1929)

The Second Sex, Simone de Beauvoir (1949)

The Golden Notebook, Doris Lessing (1962)

The Feminine Mystique, Betty Friedan (1963)

'A Bunny's Tale', Gloria Steinem (1963)

I Know Why the Caged Bird Sings, Maya Angelou (1969)

The Edible Woman, Margaret Atwood (1969)

The Dialectic of Sex: The Case for Feminist Revolution, Shulamith Firestone (1970)

The Female Eunuch, Germaine Greer (1970)

The Bluest Eye, Toni Morrison (1970)

Fear of Flying, Erica Jong (1973)

The Female Man, Joanna Russ (1975)

 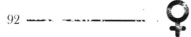

The Woman Warrior, Maxine Hong Kingston (1976)

The Women's Room, Marilyn French (1977)

Fat is a Feminist Issue, Susie Orbach (1978)

The Bloody Chamber, Angela Carter (1979)

Ain't I a Woman?, bell hooks (1981)

How To Suppress Women's Writing, Joanna Russ (1983)

The Handmaid's Tale, Margaret Atwood (1985)

Oranges Are Not the Only Fruit, Jeanette Winterson (1985)

The Creation of Patriarchy, Gerda Lerner (1986)

Gender Trouble, Judith Butler (1990)

The Beauty Myth, Naomi Wolf (1991)

Feminism and the Mastery of Nature, Val Plumwood (1993)

Persepolis, Marjane Satrapi (2000)

Female Chauvinist Pigs, Ariel Levy (2005)

Living Dolls, Natasha Walter (2010)

How to Be a Woman, Caitlin Moran (2011)

We Should All Be Feminists, Chimamanda Ngozi Adichie (2014)

Everyday Sexism, Laura Bates (2014)

Not That Kind of Girl, Lena Dunham (2014)

Men Explain Things to Me, Rebecca Solnit (2014)

If you're interested in finding out more
about our books, find us on Facebook at
SUMMERSDALE PUBLISHERS and follow
us on Twitter at **@SUMMERSDALE**.

WWW.SUMMERSDALE.COM